HOW TO BUILD AN ADVISORY BOARD TO GROW YOUR BUSINESS AND INCREASE YOUR PROFITS

By, The Advisory Board Group

DEDICATION

Dedicated to all of the entrepreneurs out there…to borrow from Steve Job's:

"Here's to the crazy ones, the misfits, the rebels, the troublemakers, the round pegs in the square holes... the ones who see things differently -- they're not fond of rules... You can quote them, disagree with them, glorify or vilify them, but the only thing you can't do is ignore them because they change things... they push the human race forward, and while some may see them as the crazy ones, we see genius, because the ones who are crazy enough to think that they can change the world, are the ones who do.

Table of Contents

Chapter I

Why Every Entrepreneur and Business Owner Should Read This Book...

Entrepreneur, Business Owner, CEO, Owner, Founder...we are all trailblazers, determined to do it our way, on our terms.

I think this book is useful because it was written by an entrepreneur, who works with entrepreneurs and lives and breathes this stuff every day. This is not meant to be a magic answer to growing your business, fixing your business or saving your business. This book is meant to fill a gap. There is very little published on this topic, and it has served as a valuable part of so many businesses.

As for my story, the value of an advisory board was realized in a very informal way during my first entrepreneurial venture. Usually, advisors are friends, associates, mentors who do not need a formal title, nor do they ask for compensation. They do it because they want to pass something on, help someone who reminds them of themselves, stay busy and connected. This is phenomenal if you can have people like this in your life, but only if they are really able to add value to your business. There are plenty of well-meaning friends and family who would like to "advise" on your business, but that doesn't make them qualified or even competent necessarily.

This book is meant to serve as a guide to attracting, contacting and hiring a real advisor, or multiple advisors that participate in growing/saving/selling your business that actually know what they are doing. Folks that have a rolodex, or the right connections, or the experience necessary to contribute real value…and you compensate them in return. It's the only way this equation really works.

In 2009 when this book concept came together, I was working on a concept for matching business owners with advisors. It was like match.com meets business and advisory boards. I had just finished a successful exit from a company I had built with a partner/founder over the course of 3 years. We had built this company from the ground up and converted 2005 revenues of $500,000 to over $12M in 2009. We built local operating companies on the ground in Africa. We had locations in NYC, London, Netherlands, Dubai and Nigeria.

We accomplished all of this in less than three years, building the company from the ground up. Although this may seem like a tremendous achievement on its own, in truth, I was not satisfied with the results. From the beginning, there was friction between the primary founder and me over the strategic growth of the company, how the company should be run, leadership styles, etc. At the core of the friction, I think it was simply a matter of us having different visions for the direction of the company and how to make the company scalable. Regardless, in 2010 it was time to move on to the next phase in my life and create something of my own and/or with partners who were more closely aligned with achieving the potential that I knew was possible.

During the course of building the company and the process of exiting the company, I realized the potential benefits of advisors. I was part of Vistage International, an organization that brings together CEOs/executives once a month to discuss various matters about their companies, strategy etc. This is where the first concept of advisory board meetings began to have tangible value for me. This was in 2007, and as a result, I began to discuss forming our own company advisory board with my business partners.

We began speaking to various candidates about joining our board and in many cases took advice from these folks directly as we were discussing the potential board seats. As we were selling into the markets of Africa, and the Middle East, in many cases, it was very difficult to penetrate these markets and win deals. We found that by bringing on local advisors from these markets, we were not only able to win more deals, but in many cases, it gave us direct access to key decision-makers in other markets as well. After achieved over $2M in revenue, we realized that the strategy that got us from 500K to $2M was not going to be the same strategy that would take us from $2M to $10M+.

The more I thought about the value of advisors, the more I became intrigued with the idea that all small businesses should have a board. The value of an advisory board was essential in my mind and virtually every small business owner I knew in the NYC area did NOT have one!

This is where the original idea for the Advisory Board Group stemmed from. Our concept was to create a team of advisors that we could make available to small businesses who were looking for board members. Of course, this was assuming that small businesses were looking for board members…and the research began.

What we found was that most small businesses:

√ Do not have a board

√ Do not realize the benefits of a board

√ Do not know how to form a board

√ Do not know where to find or how to qualify the RIGHT advisors

√ Do not know how to run a board, extract maximum value from that board

This presented a serious problem for our business matching concept. In order to sell such a service, the customer must have a need. The issue with Advisory Boards is that most "customers" do not know they have a need. Therefore, without some educational element, there would be no defined need and certainly no sales for our company.

There is quite a bit of content out there about the value of advisory boards, especially for medium to large businesses. But in the small business realm, such practices were scarce.

I had heard of SCORE and in fact, I visited them back in 2003 to discuss a business concept I had at the time. SCORE is a division of the Small Business Association (SBA) and exists to help small businesses by providing a volunteer service using veteran business professionals as mentors to small business. In theory, this makes sense, but in practice, what I found was a bit demoralizing. Although they were helpful and gave solid advice, these were not necessarily qualified for specific business advice; they were more general in their guidance. Again, I am not putting down their efforts, the service has a place, but not as a substitute to a proper advisory board.

What a small business needs are a group of seasoned advisors; each specialized in their own way, who is dedicated to helping the business owner or CEO achieve the goals of the business. They typically come with lots of relevant contacts, experience, specializations and in many cases, cash to invest if the company gets to a point worthwhile of investment. They are typically awarded some form of equity piece or profit share as this aligns them with the long-term success of the company. The power of many minds, especially at the strategic level of a company is invaluable. To not have such a structure in place is doing the company, its shareholders and its employees a disservice. This is a well-known fact, but typically overlooked in the startup, small business realm.

What's in This Book:

This book is a compilation of information about advisory boards and how to make the most effective use out of them. This book was written as a guide for entrepreneurs and small business owners throughout the world. The principles can be applied universally. The concept is simple, however, putting a board into practice is more difficult. This is the reason for writing this book. We scc an opportunity to fill a void for business owners and entrepreneurs who are interested in building advisory boards but aren't clear on how to do it and how to make the most use out of it.

2018 update: Since the first version of this book was put together in 2010, I have built several other businesses, with experiences that should be the subject of another book. The business advisor matching concept was a great idea but could not figure out how to monetize it. In the end, it was an advisor that came to be a mentor that advised me on the time to cut it off and move on with other ventures. I founded a clean energy company in 2010 after writing this book and literally followed the advice from the book that I had authored. Leveraging advisors in multiple areas of the business, I was able to build this company and command a $10M valuation by 2013. We took venture capital in 2014 with the help of an advisor and built structured finance product to raise further capital in 2015/16 using a team of advisors. The business is in the process of being acquired today, again using advisors in key areas to get it done. I have since founded another company and in the process of building a very powerful advisory board at this time.

I have intended to update this book on a regular basis based on real results, but I am only getting to it now as I have been building businesses using much of the advice in this book ever since writing it. In the meantime, I hope you find this book to be valuable as a guide to increasing the value of your business or helping you achieve whatever you desire.

Please note that I am also not naming myself, nor naming any of the contributors to this book. It is meant to be a guidebook, something practical for business owners. It is not meant to be self-promotional, or a method to build my personal brand. It is meant to be helpful, and I really hope that the value exceeds the price of this book.

Good luck!

Arthur W.B.

The Advisory Board Group

Boston MA

CHAPTER II

THE POWER OF MANY MINDS

What It Is and How It Will Work For You

What is an Advisory Board?

There are a few ways to define an advisory board.

According to Entrepreneur.com, an advisory board is:

A group of individuals who've been selected to help advise a business owner regarding any number of business issues, including marketing, sales, financing, expansion and so on; a body that advises the board of directors and management of a corporation but does not have authority to vote on corporate matters

(http://www.entrepreneur.com/encyclopedia/term/82088.html, 2010).

Our definition: An Advisory Board is a strategically selected group of individuals whose experience, expertise and ideas serve to collectively advise the business owner or business manager on the strategic direction and planning of the firm.

The primary elements include;

- Strategic Advice
- Specialized Advisors (in a function)

- Serving the owner/manager or board of the business

- Minimal liability as compared to a board of directors

In other words:

- A board of advisors is to a business owner as a mentor is to a mentee

A board of advisors is your personal sounding board, dedicated to making your business a success

All businesses, large and small must have some form of strategic direction, a plan and execution of the plan to achieve any form of success in their business. The board of advisors serves the owner or head of the company and advises on the most fundamental aspects of the business. Your board is like your foundation and effects of an effective board will be evident throughout the organization.

The primary importance of an advisory board is for the entrepreneur, owner or manager to receive the input and advice of an experienced and accomplished support team who is dedicated to making your business grow and succeed in its goals. An additional benefit is that an advisory board does not carry the liabilities, and expenses that they may experience with a more formal board of directors.

As a powerful management tool employed for and by the business, an advisory board is as unique in its nature and scope as the needs of the enterprise for which it is created.

Advisory Board vs. Board of Directors

An advisory board is an independent and external body and has no formal authority or fiduciary responsibility to your business. Because of this it offers a multitude of benefits not found in a standard management setup or from your corporate directors. Below are some comparisons to help you gain a better understanding of the benefits of an advisory board vs. a board of directors.

1. **Brainstorm!** An advisory team is a terrific platform to fearlessly test ideas, brainstorm and innovation. Advisors are a great sounding board for entrepreneurs and chief executives who want to explore tentative plans and see how their ideas resonate before pitching them to co-managers or a more formidable board of directors who evaluate their performance or compensation or may have an ax to grind. Your advisors can truly 'hear you out' and express views without being subjective.

2. **Objective "Outside" Perspective**: Benefit from experts with an outside perspective. Managers and entrepreneurs can get trapped in the day-to-day affairs of their business that they may not 'see the forest from the trees'. When you are constantly in the thick of it, it is difficult to maintain a macro perspective on your business. As you are aware, the rate of change in the business environment is faster than ever and maintaining a clear perspective is important to your strategy and success. Advisors can be your business's mirror and offer a neutral, accurate and perhaps a longer ranged perspective to help you make accurate decisions.

3. **Short Term Board**: You can compartmentalize your advisors more easily than your directors. Board directors have a responsibility to the shareholders and so that is their primary objective. In contrast, your advisory board has a responsibility to you and your business objectives. Therefore, they can be tasked to focus on specific business activities that need more attention or expertise. In many cases, you can create a short-term advisory board to help you enhance social media marketing and dissolve it after 6 months. This allows you to be able to 'compartmentalize' information with your advisors and opt to not reveal specific trade secrets, product information, or financial details.

4. **Better Value:** A board of advisors will likely cost less than a board of directors, however you can achieve similar benefits. Directors are typically compensated more with salary, profit share, stocks or stock options, and you may also need to pay each time they attend a meeting. Advisory boards, on the other hand, are a great way for you to enjoy the benefits of a supportive board at a fraction of the cost.

Most advisors are not chiefly motivated by money when joining advisory boards. They usually place higher value on other benefits, such as: recognition, networking opportunities, experience, resume/CV building, and contribution or simply to keep themselves busy and give back to the small business community.

You can compensate your advisory board in a number of different ways and we will get to that in a bit, but suffice it to say that costs are substantially lower than keeping a board of directors or hiring management consultants.

5. **Easier:** Finally maintaining an advisory board requires less cost in terms of time, effort and training. Although you can choose to make your meetings as formal, as you would like, you can also make them relatively informal. With some guidance and some practice, you can learn how to effectively run your board and maximize your results.

Does My Business Need One?

It all depends on you and your business!

There are many examples of successful entrepreneurs, businesses and chief executives. But how did they achieve such success? How did their businesses grow and achieve so much?

There are many books written on the topics of success, so we will not go too deep on this one, but we can tell you for sure that they did not accomplish such success all on their own.

The real question comes down to you: Can you be open to advice and suggestion? Are you able to put in the necessary time to develop board agendas and analyze key business issues in an open and candid format?

These are the primary questions you must ask yourself. Many entrepreneurs are very headstrong and do not easily take direction or advice. In these cases, an advisory board may be a waste of your time as well as your advisors time.

So, if you can open your mind to the advice, suggestions and expertise of those who have been there and done it before, your business may in fact, benefit immensely from an advisory board.

So much can be earned (and learned) from choosing to share part of the burden of your business to a well chosen, dedicated advisory board.

Most entrepreneurial experts recommend having a board (if you can handle it) and more and more startups, midsized, and large corporations are utilizing this powerful resource.

Business owners who singlehandedly run their enterprise or manage it with a few peers usually find themselves short of three things: time, energy, and support.

Having a team of strategic advisors allows you to save or buy back some of these important resources.

1. An Advisory Board Saves You Time

Every entrepreneur knows the all too common dilemma of "wearing all of the hats" leaving little to no time for anything else. So what goes to the wayside? The important things like, family, education, vacations and exercise take a backseat as you continue to become more and more consumed in the activities of your business. A lot of this is due to your weaknesses in one or more of the functions of your business.

By forming your own advisory board you can save yourself valuable time:

- ➢ Your advisory board can advise you on areas where you are weak and potentially increase your efficiency in those areas.
- ➢ Advisors are often well-connected members in your industry or in their industry. You can get access to their business contacts, get introduced to connections and associations they are affiliated with, and obtain referrals.

> Save yourself years of experimentation and trial-and-error by learning from your advisors' mistakes so you never have to do them yourself.

2. Energize your business

Because of its collaborative nature, an advisory board allows you to achieve more results with less work, making your business more efficient and productive. Imagine the confidence that can be achieved when you are relying on both your intuition and the advice of your board.

> You can make better and more accurate decisions by utilizing the collective viewpoints and expertise of your board members.
> You can entrust your team to help you with the important things like working *on* your business and not just *in* your business.

3. Your Advisors Support You

Your advisory team will be there for you through both good and difficult times and will be your best source for honest, unbiased feedback. They can also help you:

> ➢ Avert isolation as you are able to access your advisors regularly and sometimes even beyond scheduled meetings when you need them.
> ➢ Get honest opinions and advice from people who have a genuine interest in your business.
> ➢ Add immediate value and credibility to your company from the combined support and prestige of your board members.

4. Act as if!

Large companies have boards, why not you? Where do you want to take your business? Are you satisfied with simply getting by or do you want to create a sustainable and saleable business?

Consider the real-life advisory board of a small software development company.

- o A Technical Director for a midsized but well-known technology firm
- o A corporate lawyer affiliated with a Fortune 500 corporation
- o A marketing and brand management expert for software products
- o A former CEO from a sizeable firm specializing in embedded systems

Imagine what it would cost you to hire these experts to work for your company!

Surprisingly, many experts with similar profiles are quite happy, and some even flattered, to be even just considered for an active role in your business.

You can build yourself a dream team of exceptional advisors and by compensating them with small equity stakes or stock options earned over time, you all share in the rewards.

And keep in mind that your advisors are free from the fiduciary responsibilities that come with a board of director's seat, which makes the advisor position that much more attractive.

But….I'm just a start up!

So what?!

As a start up, the best time to start acting like a serious business is right away.

There are a number of things that should be set up before you launch such as;

- o   Business plan
- o   Shareholder agreement
- o   Management structure (even if you have 0 employees right now) Read The E-Myth Revisited for reference
- o   Your finances and accounting books
- o   Company formation, bank account

Begin with a Board!

What we are suggesting is that board formation (Advisory Boards) are just as important, in fact, we would recommend beginning with a board of advisors who can guide you through the pre-startup phase. This will help with all of the foundational decisions that most are unsure of when they start a business.

So what does such a board provide?: *Instant leverage with minimal investment.*

There is no reason not to apply leverage right from the startup phase onward.

Creating an impressive advisory board can guarantee to provide startups with

- ✓ Instant credibility and value for your startup that makes you appear more reliable and thus investment and credit worthy
- ✓ Instant contacts and doors to important connections that can be potential sources of funding or new customers
- ✓ Tons of advice, guidance and expertise at minimal cost.
- ✓ Strengthen fund raising credibility

Startup Board:

A start up board should consist of 2-4 advisors. Ideally, the board members have bought into the concept and business and will participate at no charge during your first 3-6 months. You can offer a small equity stake to make it worth their time if you are unable to compensate them right away. Or offer them a cash incentive to be paid once the company is profitable. This provides upside for success and does not carry the costs of borrowing capital at interest rates of 10%+.

Once the board is in place, aside from scheduled meetings, you can also get in touch with members for questions and advice as needed.

Startup Advisors:

Advisors for startup boards are generally more interested in the non-monetary benefits that the position offers them. They understand you can't compensate them with cash, but are happy to serve your company for the following reasons:

- To give back to your business and the small business community
- Increase their own experience and qualifications
- Further expand their connections and contacts
- Get a ground floor equity stake in a promising company

Start Small and Short:

As a startup you may wish to just test the waters with your advisory board. Once in place, you will be able to gauge what is working and what is not. This is a great opportunity for you to 'test-drive' your advisors by issuing short-term, as opposed to long-term goals, and limiting their term to a few months. This will allow you to evaluate the board with minimal commitment and motivate the advisors to perform effectively.

But... I Just Have a Small Business

Advisory boards can work wonders on any type or size of business, and most experts agree it is particularly useful for young, growing companies.

Most small businesses do not have a large management team, in many cases, the single entrepreneur is doing it all.

While such activity can be empowering and strengthen your ability as a businessperson, you will also have apparent weaknesses. These weaknesses can be offset by a group of experts and peers who have an interest in the company and whom you can call upon to provide moral support and fresh points of view. Advisory boards allow the busy and oftentimes overwhelmed entrepreneurs to *unburden* themselves by receiving the levelheaded guidance of an outside advisor.

Does my small business need an advisory board?

That depends. Where is your business right now?
Are these familiar?

o Has your business stagnated? Reached a plateau and stopped growing?

o Heading downhill? A business that fails to grow is dying

o Early days? Overwhelmed?

o Feeling like an employee of your own business?

o Ready for expansion?

o Ready for merge, acquisition or to sell/exit?

o Going public?

No matter how much experience you have as a business owner, as your company grows, you will inevitably reach critical points that require strategic thought, advice, plans and execution.

Whatever your plans are for your business, it makes sense to have a board in place to help you through the process and all that comes along with it.

Real-Life Advisory Boards @ Work

Advisory boards are experiencing tremendous popularity in recent decades, and with the whirlwind evolution of the Internet coupled by exponential changes and challenges in global business trends, more and more companies, large or small, are utilizing the power of advisors to help them thrive and grow.

Consider some recent highlights in the employment and progress of advisory boards in various sized companies from early 2009:

1. Apple co-founder joins TechForEducators.com's Advisory Board. Steve Wozniak, inventor of the personal computer, joined TechForEducators.com's advisory board in May 2009. TechForEducators.com sells educational software and hardware products to educators, and works with the Kids In Need Foundation to give US$1.25 of free school supplies to impoverished students for every $1 worth of products sold. Wozniak admits he has "a better place at smaller companies looking at new ideas," and has devoted his recent years to various business and philanthropic ventures with a particular

focus on educational technology. (Source: TechForEducators.com)

2. Media content veteran joins startup company Box. In July 2009, David L. Simon, who has held senior executive positions for DreamWorks Animation, Fox Television Station Group and Disney among others, joined the advisory board of Israel-based new media and content creation company The Box. Simon provides strategic consultation for the company in content for broadcast entertainment and advertising. (Source: The Box Ltd Press Release)

3. Wikipedia and CK-12. Online encyclopedia group Wikipedia welcomed CK-12 chair Neeru Khosla into the former's advisory board in January 2009. In July, Wikipedia and Wikia co-founder Jimmy Wales became adviser for CK-12, a nonprofit which has pioneered the offering of 'open source textbooks" online to educators and kindergarten to grade 12 students. (Source: CK-12 Foundation)

4. Craigslist Founder Joins Wikimedia Advisory Board. Craig Newmark joined the advisory group for the nonprofit that runs Wikipedia in November 2009. Wikimedia Foundation said it chose Newmark, who founded Craigslist in 1995, because of his work as an innovator and evangelist and his understanding of Web-based communities. Other members of Wikimedia's board, put together in 2007, are Electronic Frontier Foundation co-founder Mitch Kapor, venture capitalist Roger McNamee, and CK-12 chair Neeru Khosla. Wikimedia says the board serves as "a mechanism for input from leaders and thinkers in fields such as education, technology, and free culture" and convene once a year. (Source: Wikimedia Foundation Press Release)

5. Condoleezza Rice joins Startup C3. In December 2009, stealth energy startup C3 LLC named Condoleezza Rice as member of its advisory board and also raised almost $26 million in funding. Founded by Thomas Siebel, who founded Siebel Systems, C3 provides energy and emissions management to corporations. Also on its advisory board are

Senator and Secretary of Energy Spencer Abraham. (Source: Crunchbase.com)

6. Facebook's Safety Advisory Board. Also in December last year, the world's top social networking site formed an advisory group composed of 5 Internet safety organizations – ConnectSafely, WiredSafety, Common Sense Media, Childnet International, and The Family Online Safety Institute – to review its users' current safety resources and seek advice on overall best practices for safety. Facebook added the board is part of efforts to rid the site of registered sex offenders. (Source: Facebook Press Release)

7. Voyager Capital. The Seattle-based venture brought Bruce Chizen, former CEO of Adobe Systems, into its advisory board in September last year. In January 2010, it welcomed Steve Singh, chairman and chief executive of Redmond, WA-based software firm Concur Technologies, on its board. Concur Technologies focuses on corporate travel and expense management. (Source: Voyager Capital News)

8. SVTC. The privately owned semiconductor solutions provider in San Jose, California announced in January 2010 its Advisory Board and initial members who are recognized leaders in the semiconductor industry. The board's charter is to provide guidance in the company's technology development and long-term roadmap and assess relevant technology and industry trends. (Source: SVTC Press Release)

9. Sypris Electronics. Also last month, the Tampa Florida based subsidiary of Louisville-based Sypris Solutions Inc. created a senior cyber-security board to help the company understand the nation's cyber and information-security needs. The company provides electronics engineering and manufacturing services primarily for the defense and aerospace industries. (Source: Sypris Electronics Press Release)

10. WellTek. In February 2010, Florida based health company WellTek established a Medical Advisory Board for its

wholly-owned subsidiary, Pure HealthyBack, to institute and lead the most important step in healthcare reform for chronic neck and back pain - measuring and reporting of patient results. The members of the Advisory Board include five leading medical experts in the US. (Source: PR Newswire)

These are just a few examples of thousands of companies who look to their advisory boards for strategy, support and advice, in ensuring the success and continued growth of their businesses.

Fortunately, we have come to the best part of this book, which is where we start to plan and create your own unique, incredible powerhouse of an advisory board, whether you are a startup, a small company or a midsized business. Building your own dream team of advisors is an incredibly exciting endeavor fit only for the most dedicated entrepreneur who seeks to strengthen his or her business. Ready to begin?

CHAPTER III

THE BUILDING BLOCKS

10 KEYS to Creating Your Unique Advisory Board

The Direction of Your Business

<u>What's Your Status?</u>

The very first step in creating your advisory board is to understand where your business is at this particular point.

Your good ol' SWOT analysis!

Enumerating all the strengths and weaknesses (internal factors), and opportunities and threats (external factors) to your business is tremendously useful in assessing any current business situation and whenever you need to make a major decision or embark on a new project.

What could the business improve?

SWOT allows you to analyze almost every aspect of your business and facilitate a flow of ideas and answers to the questions that follow. As a business owner or manager, do you need to?

- Improve, expand or change a product or service?
- Increase or improve sales and customer experience?
- Streamline operations and/or improve processes?

- Increase production, investment or acquisition?

- Design, market and/or effectively launch a new product or service?

- Minimize costs, expand or downsize, manage finance?

- Boost your company's image or brand, enter new markets or territories?

This exercise will generate a clear picture of the areas in your enterprise that require attention.

Your Board's Purpose

Now that you have determined the specific needs of your business, you can now define the best purpose and mission for your advisory board. The worst you can do at this point is to start an advisory board without knowing where it should help you.

At this stage, decide whether your board will fulfill any, a combination, or all of the following:

- Provide expert, fearless and objective advice and strategies

- Boost your company's value, image, credit-worthiness, or credibility.

- Increase your network, connections and alliances

- Open new markets and opportunities and/or increase your customer base

Equally important is defining who the advisory board will advise. Will it be you (the entrepreneur/business owner), the CEO, another senior executive or your board of directors or management team?

Your company and advisors must both understand in which area advice will be sought and to whom this will be given.

Forming Your Board's Charter

The Free Online dictionary defines charter as "a document outlining the conditions under which a corporation or other corporate body is organized and defining its rights and privileges."

Once you have determined what your advisory board is created for and what it needs to do, it is time to draft its charter.

Your board's charter will incorporate answers to such questions as:

- What is your advisory board and what is its mission?
- What and how will the board accomplish its mission and objectives?
- What are the board's rights and privileges?
- What are the functions of board members?
- What are the members' terms, duties, compensation and liabilities?

The great thing about your charter is you can always change or add to it as you convene, evaluate and review the goals and performance of your advisory group.

Forming your board's charter is crucial – but it does not need to be long. Because an advisory board is a less formal group and has very few, if any, liabilities and no fiduciary duties, you can cover the basics in the charter at the onset of creating your board and modify or expand it to cover subsequent terms and agreements. The shorter and simpler your charter is, the better.

As a disclaimer, do not forget to involve a lawyer to make sure you cover all the necessary legal issues. In our experience, we have found that rocket lawyer (google it) is super inexpensive and simple to use for any contracts.

Choosing Your Advisory Board Model

Advisory boards in general are either of two types: *ad hoc* or *standing*.

You have already decided what your board will accomplish. Is their mission geared towards special tasks or business activities? Or will they serve to be your sounding board for the long term?

Ad hoc boards, as opposed to standing advisory groups, are usually employed when the business needs:

➢ To implement a short-term project that requires special input, skills or resources of particular individuals from specialized fields. Examples: new market campaigns, product development, scientific projects, an event launch, and regional conferences.

➢ To demonstrate credibility quickly in a particular environment or field. When a company decides to expand into a new territory, for instance, advisors may be employed to help the company immerse itself easily and implement a successful local presence.

That said, no advisory board is exactly like another. There are many different kinds of advisory boards as there are companies and the reasons they need strategies and expertise in specific areas of their business.

Below are some examples of advisory boards that serve various organizations and business today:

1. **Executive Advisory Boards**: A common advisory board model used by startups, small businesses, family-owned companies, and midsized to large organizations alike. The board offers general advice and strategies to management executives or directors within the company.

2. **Scientific Advisory Boards:** Companies value the scientific expertise and experience of scientists, research experts, and medical luminaries and form advisory boards to explore leading edge research and development in various areas of science and healthcare.

3. **Technology Advisory Boards**: Technology boards are highly popular and are formed to guide and inform organizations on the latest technological trends, developments, and develop new and improved strategies, products and processes.

4. **International Advisory Boards**: These boards are created for companies to manage international growth, expansion, global operations and services.

5. **Nonprofit Advisory Boards**: Nonprofits take on experienced individuals into their advisory board to help them conduct various activities for the benefit of the general public without profit.

6. **Marketing Advisory Boards**: Advisory boards can also help companies venture and expand successfully into new territories, markets or services. Some types of marketing focused advisory boards are those set up to strategize for new markets, brand management, or web marketing.

7. **Social Media Advisory Boards**: These boards are a new trend and are created to help companies formulate strategies to enhance their social media activities.

8. **Futures Advisory Boards**: Businesses can better anticipate unexpected events and prepare for the future with the help of a group of experienced advisors.

9. **Customer Advisory Boards**: These boards are formed to enhance the efforts and performance of a company's sales force. Advisors can also counsel on recent market trends and design effective strategies to adapt to growing change.

10. **Virtual Advisory Boards**: More a distinction in structure than purpose, virtual boards are becoming highly popular in today's business environments and with the evolution of the Internet. Virtual boards are a diversified group of individuals serving as advisors from anywhere across the globe using technologies such as web conferences and emails.

How Big or How Small?

There is no general consensus on the ideal advisory board size.

Just as each business varies distinctly from others in terms of size and complexity, so will the size and mandate of each advisory board. A small company may have 3-4 people on board; a midsized business may have 5 to 7, while large organizations may have 8 or more advisors.

A common advice among startups and small businesses however is: Start small and modify as your needs change.

Forbes.Com notes smaller companies with no more than 20 employees usually have up to three advisors, according to the National Federation of Independent Business. In the same article, Richard Magid, president of SoundBoard, a consultancy that specializes in creating and running advisory boards, suggests an odd number is good when you need a vote on key decisions.

Starting with a few members allows you to maximize the expertise and contribution of each individual. For small businesses, an advisory board of 3 members is a great start. More than 6 or 8 advisors are usually deemed too many.

The Brains You Should Bring "On Board"

Each member of your advisory team fills a specific role or a combination of vital roles. Some may carry out defined tasks and results. Others can supply excellent contacts or connect you to networks that are valuable to your business. Some are selected for their expertise and the input they can provide. Other members may be there to lend their name or status because this would be an important marketing or investment tool for your organization.

When putting your board together, look at them as a team rather than as individual experts. The group as a whole should be able to work successfully together. The people you select should be open to new ideas, differing viewpoints and constructive feedback. Ideal advisors are also flexible and accommodating of differences. Also make sure your advisors are committed to give reasonable time to your business and to carry out the tasks expected of them. This requires proper communication to each board member of his or her roles and duties.

So, who should you bring on board? Below are several unique individuals that could help your business grow exponentially and would be great assets to any advisory board.

a. **The Financial Whiz**: A financial expert is a *must* in any committee or board. For a standing group who will serve your company as an ongoing think tank, or even for short term projects that have financial considerations, bring in someone who specializes in finance or investment, or is trained in offering counsel in financial investments such as stocks, bonds, and insurance. Finance whizzes have different interests. Some concentrate on particular types of investments, such as securities, insurance, or real estate. There is also "financial engineering" expertise to be considered in your business model. For example, in our business selling clean power systems to offset diesel usage, we found that converting to a model more like Solar City was advantageous to the growth model, financing and enterprise value of our business.

b. **The Legal Expert**: You need a lawyer or a legal advocate who can give you advice about legal matters. Most business dealings require a legal point of view, and in particular, where contracts, trademarks, patents and copyrights are and other legal rights are required. Choose which kinds of legal experience would be most helpful to achieving your advisory board's charter.

c. **The Specialist**: At various stages in your business, you may need specialist consultants such as a management consultant, a sales or marketing expert, or a scientific and technology expert. They may or may not form a permanent part of your advisory board, this depends on your type of business and your goals, but it can be useful to call them in to give you specialized advice in areas that that you, your managers, directors or other advisors lack.

d. **A Who's Who**: Sometimes you may be looking less for advice and more for added value, credibility or an instant image boost to your business. In this case you need to select key individuals in your industry or community who have established profiles and powerful contacts and collaborations that can empower your business. These people may expand your network, allow you to access more sources of investment, or establish your business in the market. They also may not necessarily come from a similar background as you or your business. Although high profile individuals are extremely busy, if chosen well they will be able to contribute to your advisory group and make a reasonable amount of commitment to your business.

e. **A Key Customer or Supplier**: Depending on your board's mandate, you may also benefit from bringing in a valuable customer or key supplier as advisors on your team. For instance, a supplier can help in ad hoc boards set up for product development. Key customers can provide direct and highly valuable input in customer advisory boards or if your board will focus on strengthening sales and customer operations. Customer or supplier advisors should sign a non-disclosure agreement (NDA) to protect your company's privacy and key information.

The web is currently one of the most powerful resources for searching and finding these experts and leading-edge innovators in every field, industry and community imaginable. Do a web search for your target names and profiles. Linkedin.com is another great resource. Conduct a comprehensive research on their details, interests, and accomplishments.

You can also consult your contacts, mentors, other business leaders, your local chamber of commerce, business associations, even friends and relatives – who may know key people that would be perfect for your team. Getting recommendations from people you know also increase your chances of obtaining personal introductions to the names on your wish list.

Do not forget to also note and seek out candidates as you attend or conduct seminars, conferences and exhibits.

Choosing your ideal advisors is at the core of your advisory board project. This step requires strategic selection and evaluation. You will be creating a mix of different people, expertise and backgrounds and expect them to work successfully together and individually to strengthen your goals and vision. Take enough time to assess your prospects and determine who will make it to your elite dream team.

Creating Structure & Expectations

At this point, you've already determined your advisory board's charter or purpose. You have also defined your company's expectations of how the board should help you. And finally, you have decided which profiles fit into your board. You may already be entertaining names of people you know that you think would be perfect for your team.

It's now time to set more specific expectations and structure for the group and its prospect members.

Defining Board Meetings

How Often?

Determine the frequency of board meetings that would be most effective for your board. Quarterly meetings work well for most companies. However, if you are a new business, have issues that are frequent and require more attention, or if your board is a special task group, then it is advisable to schedule monthly meetings at this particular stage of the project or business.

Start with a target week and day in a month or quarter to schedule meetings; you can certainly adjust dates as and when your board convenes.

Where and By What Means?

Will the meetings involve face-to-face discussions over breakfast or lunch at your company's premises? Will your board meet once per quarter over dinner at a high-end restaurant? Will you schedule intermittent virtual/video conferencing to save resources and time?

The key to determining these factors is to consider your advisors' availability, respecting their schedules and locations, and integrating technology whenever convenient. Your advisors are likely offering their services at little or no compensation, so set reasonable expectations. Remember you need to ascertain these details before pitching your invitation to prospect board members.

How Formal and How Long Do We Convene?

You also need to define: how formal or informal are meetings going to be? How long should they be?

The level of structure in meetings, whether formal or informal, is usually up to you. This can subsequently be modified by you or your board members as more meetings are held and a specific structure proves to be effective.

General consensus on length of board meetings is between 2 and 3 hours. This ensures meetings do not dwindle and are on track. If your board meets infrequently or if there are critical issues, exceptions can be made but always ensure meetings are tight and do not waste your advisors' time.

Defining Advisor Expectations

You should be able to set clear expectations this early as to how your board should perform and how each advisor should contribute to the team.

Clearly define your rules for each advisor in terms of responsibilities, investment in time, and term of office. These details will be included in your invitation to prospective members.

In determining individual expectations, consider questions such as the following

- ➢ Do you expect the advisor to interact with you on a regular basis?
- ➢ Are you inviting the prospect member to simply add status to your company and thus not expect him or her to attend or be available for regular meetings or tasks?
- ➢ How do you expect each advisor to be available outside of scheduled meetings?
- ➢ How do you want the advisor to participate in case of crisis or emergencies? Can you call them up or expect them to be available in urgent situations?
- ➢ What is each board member accountable for and are they going to be responsible for certain tasks?
- ➢ Are they required to oversee and manage implementation of specific projects?
- ➢ Will they be privy to private information and thus bound to non-disclosure?

Keep'em Coming and Going

There is no standard term for advisors to serve on your board however the smart way is to keep each advisor's term short but renewable.

Recruit board members ideally on 12 to 24 month terms, according to experts.

Some benefits of keeping advisors' terms short are

- ✓ If you are a startup you have greater freedom in keeping or dissolving the advisory board based on your needs and available resources.
- ✓ If you are a small business, you can choose to keep some effective members and not renew those who aren't.
- ✓ For an organization of any size, one can keep a board member's term short if the advisor is required to contribute only towards a short-term project or activity e.g. scientific or technological development, expansion, legal disputes etc.

✓ You can keep value adding members and part with non-performing advisors without having to 'fire' them or carry out awkward dismissals.

How to Compensate?

Many advisors sit on boards for free, but experts say about 20% of small businesses and startups pay their advisory board members.

We recommend that you compensate and provide your advisors with certain incentives or perks that would keep them motivated and interests aligned. If you can align their success to your success, all vectors are pointing in the right direction.

The amount of compensation usually depends on whom you are inviting and how involved you would like them to be. The bigger your company, and the greater the contribution expected from the advisor, the greater you are expected to offer your prospective board member.

You can pay your advisors in any combination of the following:

Per-Meeting Honorarium.

Many small and medium sized companies pay their board members per meeting, some from as little as $100 each, and many between $300 and $500 per advisor per meeting. Large companies usually pay as high as a few thousand dollars per member for each meeting.

Annual Retainer.

Some advisory boards pay annual compensation instead of per meeting fees, usually from $1000 and more per year. For this, you should expect attendance and participation in regular meetings, and unlimited access via phone or email for advice. Some advisory boards are paid an annual stipend plus payment for each meeting attended.

Food, Travel and Events.

Companies usually provide complimentary lunches, dinners i.e. food and drink in advisory board meetings and cover the board members' travel and out-of-pocket expenses. You can also provide and pay for special events and expect to reimburse advisors for long distance travel and other miscellaneous costs.

Non-Monetary Benefits.

You can also compensate board members by reciprocating their service – you can be a member of their advisory board (if this is of value to them). You could also offer other benefits like offering to help with a certain program or project in their own organization or business, volunteering or donating to their chosen non-profit, offering them preferential offers if they are a customer, or recommending their business to your own contacts. Be careful not to overstretch yourself however. As a business owner, you need to be focused primarily on your business. Any time spent elsewhere is time NOT spent on your business.

Discounts and Gift Certificates.

You can also give out discount coupons and gift vouchers to your board members as added perks. Get creative!

Stocks or Stock Options.

Giving your advisors a slice of equity in your business is also an option. This compensation is usually employed by companies who expect significant and measured results from their advisors and where the business has something tangible to provide. Providing equity has become common to startup culture, but all too many times, it is never realized. The advisors have to really believe in your business and that they can help to find the equity valuable.

Equity is an attractive offer to any potential advisor that can see the value and usually issued at between 0.25% to 3% of your common stock. But be sure to structure it in such a way that there are expectations and incentives for your board member to continually add value to your board and company. Also, if you have investors and a formal board of directors, this should be discussed with them.

Try providing performance-based or results-based stock and bonuses instead to ensure you get the most from your advisors and do not waste precious equity on those who do not deliver or lose interest after the initial enthusiasm. If you wish to give out equity, tie it with targets that each advisor should achieve to be able to obtain a % of ownership in your business.

This means that you don't give equity away on day one. You allow them to earn in or "vest" over a time period. Let's say you are willing to provide 1% equity over 3 years, vesting at 0.25% per year and the final 0.25% vesting at the end of the term. This locks in 3 year's worth of this advisor's time, while also providing a healthy 1% of the company to them in return. If they are not performing, you can fire them in 1 year and they will only own 0.25% at that time. Similarly, if they are not seeing the value or potential, they can also walk away. But if they see the value, and the company is growing, they will be very motivated to add as much value as they can to earn in their 1% over the course of the 3 years.

Above all, keep in mind when defining each member's compensation structure that your advisors benefit in many other ways than just compensation, including expanding their network and meeting new prospects, contacts and partners; learning new strategies and technologies from other board members; broadening their resume and status; and contributing to a worthwhile cause.

The Invitation

So why should someone want to be an advisor for you?

You need to employ great selling skills to get an outstanding YES from the people you want on your dream team and answer the all-important question of: What's In It for Them?

Just like any sales strategy, it's important to know your prospects well and understand what would convince them to join your board.

As they say, "different strokes for different folks." If you desire to recruit a high-profile individual, you will need to focus on benefits other than compensation; if you are inviting someone who is fresh from his or her MBA, then you can highlight the advantages of increasing his or her network contacts and experience.

As most of the people you would want to invite are either busy or have their own activities and businesses to run, ensure that your invitation is succinct but compelling.

The Invitation Letter:

You should only send your invitation letter when you are 100% sure you want the prospect to be part of your advisory board. This requires whittling down your wish list of advisors and contacting only those you believe to be the 'best of the best'. And remember contact only a few or you could end up with too many people saying 'yes' and having to reject them.

The first part of your letter should start by complimenting the individual for their expertise and success, and/or of the organization or company they own or lead. It should also mention your purpose to invite them to be a strategic advisor on your board.

The second part of your letter should briefly tell the story of your company, its history, vision and goals, and what it needs to grow and become more successful.

The next part should briefly detail the advisory board's mandate, goals and responsibility.

The fourth part of your letter should showcase the benefits that being an advisor on your board could offer the specific individual.

Finally, close your invite by thanking the prospect for his time, reiterating your invitation, and inviting an appointment or further queries from the invitee.

Sample Invitation Letter

Below is a template to help you generate further ideas in creating an invitation that generates excitement and a yes from your prospective members.

Introduction:

You have been recommended to our team as an exemplary and highly accomplished individual whose success and contribution to the telecommunications industry are invaluable and well renowned. We would like to invite you to consider an important role in our advisory board as Strategic Advisor.

Company Description:

Our company, Connect It Ltd, was founded in 2006 and is a successful, growing provider of telecommunications services in Chicago. Since its inception, our business has generated continual growth and profit. We are currently in the planning stage of expanding our telecoms network to new areas in Chicago and would like to seek the expertise of top innovators in the industry to help us strategize and implement our expansion project with great success.

Advisory Board Description:

We have created a Strategic Advisory Board to aid our team in creating, brainstorming and reviewing the financial, marketing and technological aspects of our network expansion project. Our board members convene for a 2-hour dinner and discussion once a month, and may respond to some follow up questions or requests for advice by email. Advisors are also privy to key information regarding our business and agree to non-disclosure.

Benefits to the Advisor:

In exchange for your invaluable input and time, we would like to offer you a $400 honorarium for each meeting to be paid directly to you or a charity of your choice. We are also happy to cover any expenses you incur from joining our advisory meetings and recommend your organization to our key contacts and suppliers. As our board currently comprises key IT experts and marketing executives in the internet services and telecommunications industries, you might also be keen to further expand your network reach and be introduced to our business and key clients.

Closing:

Many thanks for taking the time to review our invitation and we hope you would consider being a part of Connect It's Advisory Board. I would be very happy to arrange a meeting at a convenient time for you, and if you have any queries, please feel free to reach me by phone at (number) or email (email address).

The endeavor to approach top-notch individuals and key players in various industries may be outside of one's comfort zone and may generate a few no's from those individuals on your dream list.

However, all in all it is an exciting activity and can likely create more exposure for your business as you contact individuals who may not have known of you or your business previously.

CHAPTER IV

My Board is Now Set Up!

Now What?

Let's say your dream advisors have finally said yes and agreed to be part of your advisory board. Well, Congratulations! It's time to celebrate! You have just empowered your business with the best brains there are around to provide you the best strategies and connections for your business.

Here are the next steps to undertake after you have successfully recruited your advisors.

Agreements & Non-disclosures

Distribute your Advisory Board Agreement, which should include an NDA.

As mentioned in previous chapters, your advisory board members do not have fiduciary duties to your company.

A fiduciary duty is a legal or ethical relationship of trust between two or more parties, where the fiduciary or 'trustee' is expected to be completely loyal to the party (the 'principal') whom he is bound by duty.

There is no such duty in the case of a company and its advisory board. Therefore, you do need to protect your company's assets, information and secrets, and require each adviser to sign an Advisory Board Agreement.

Your agreement should also include a Non-Disclosure Agreement (NDA) that outlines confidential material or information that the parties may share but cannot be divulged to third parties. It is a contract that ensures you and your advisors do not disclose information covered by the agreement.

Your Advisory Board Agreement should ensure that each adviser agrees to:

➢ Perform the duties and functions required of an adviser such as attending meetings and carrying out duties as mandated by your advisory board for the compensation agreed.

➢ Be available for consultation and advice to the company as reasonably required.

- Serve for the term as provided in the Agreement and agree to conditions for termination.
- Substantiate all expenses covered by the company with complete and accurate documentation.
- Non-disclosure confidential agreement (NDA).
- Not withhold information from your company if he or she is involved in a competing business or commitment. Alternatively, you may also require a non- compete agreement from your advisors.
- Affirm that his or her advisory position in your company does not violate any of his or her other commitments or contracts.
- Assign any work product and invention created to the company in his or her capacity as an adviser.

You DO NOT necessarily need to hire a qualified legal expert to draft your Advisory Board Agreement. Rather, there are tons of templates out there that you can use and then simply have a lawyer sign off on it so that you are covered legally, and you minimize your expenses. Again – we highly encourage you to check out rocket lawyer!

It is also advisable to reissue confidentiality agreements to advisors upon each term renewal.

Appointing a Chairperson

Granted, you have chosen only la crème de la crème for your advisors. But will your advisory board be effective, organized, and produce great results on all tasks and projects, without assigned leaders? No Chance!

Ensure that you appoint a member to take on a key leadership role as Chairperson or President of your advisory board from the get-go. Mention this in your invitation letter and ensuing talks with the prospective member so he or she understands his or her expected position in the team.

Some companies allow advisory members to elect their own chair, but this charge should ideally be by appointment from the company.

You can also appoint a vice chairman to take over in the absence of the chairman of the board. Some companies allow advisory members to elect their own vice-chair. Again, it is advisable for the company to appoint this charge.

Your chair is the overseer of all deliverables assigned to the advisory group and chairs meetings. He can assign special tasks, form committees for specific activities, and take decisions about administration where needed.

In varying cases, board members may find a subsequent need to create other positions and elect suitable members within the group or its committees.

Choosing your board leaders early on will promote proper structure within your advisory team.

The other option is for you to chair the meetings! If you go down this route, be sure to prepare yourself for such a role as the effectiveness of your board depends on it!

Announcing the Board

Now that you've organized your team, it's time to get your advisory board working to boost your marketing & PR advantage.

Create a press release and get it published on your and other select business and press release websites and your local newspaper. Announce your newly formed advisory group, its members, their expertise and experience, as well as the structure and mandate of your board. Make your press release article customer- and investment-friendly; highlighting the benefits your advisors will contribute to enhance your service to customers, suppliers, partners and business contacts.

Also create a dedicated page on your company website announcing your advisory board's members and their profiles complete with pictures and a brief description of how their input will be utilized to benefit your advisory board and organization. Make sure to keep the page regularly updated with your advisory board's current activities and achievements.

Board Communication

a. You can create email accounts for your board members and enroll them in your company's mailing lists for regular updates and monthly newsletters.

b. Introduce your advisors to your company by sending them an introductory email, which lets them understand your company mission and vision, your business goals and why they were chosen, as well as when they can expect their first advisory board meeting.

c. Orient each adviser by email, of who the other members of the advisory board are, the board's organizational structure, and more importantly, let each adviser understand their individual roles and the tasks expected of them, so they can prepare well ahead of the advisory meeting.

d. Distribute your business plan to your advisors. This will familiarize the board with how your business is structured, how it operates and what your goals are moving forward.

e. Schedule a tour of your company premises for the advisory board or if convening them is not possible, schedule a tour for a few advisors at a time. You may also wish to add this in the agenda of your first advisory meeting if geographically feasible.

f. Outside of scheduled meetings, keep your advisors motivated and enthusiastic about your business by sending them regular updates even when they are not required to give advice or offer strategies at that particular time.

The First Meeting

You should prepare for the first meeting well in advance; at least 3 weeks.

    a. Select a date for your first advisory meeting. Ensure the date is not too far away from when your advisors were first recruited. Take advantage of your advisors' nascent enthusiasm and keep the momentum going.

    b. Select and reserve a venue that is geographically convenient for each board member if possible.

    c. Develop a comprehensive but concise agenda for your first meeting and brainstorm for topics to include in the agenda from your management team.

    d. Inform your advisors of the date and time of your first board meeting, as well as a brief description of the agenda to be discussed and any action plan(s) expected from each member or the group as a whole.

e. Determine what business information is required to support your agenda. You may need to distribute copies of your business plan, present graphs, charts, fact sheets and reports. Produce and develop the materials needed to facilitate your meeting. At least 1-2 weeks before convening your board, distribute soft copies of the relevant materials you have developed that your advisors will need to be able to participate and contribute fully to the advisory meeting.

Creating the Agenda for Your Advisory Meeting

When drafting the agenda for your first, and all subsequent advisory board meetings, keep in mind several things

✓ Identify the specific topic or topics to be discussed. These points will be incorporated in your agenda and are the basis for the meeting.

✓ Each topic on your agenda should be time bound. This allows you to ensure the meeting stays on track and efficient. Try to keep topics to an hour or less.

✓ Each discussion point, or issue should require or generate specific action plans from your board. Allot appropriate time for the board to discuss each topic in the schedule.

✓ If no conclusion or resolution is drawn after a topic has been fully discussed or has taken enough time, feel free to consider continuing ('table') the topic in the next meeting or over subsequent email, chat, or phone correspondence with advisors. This can be beneficial for decisions that need more time to be adopted and/or implemented.

✓ It is vital to record the minutes of your meeting. Assign a secretary to do so or record or videotape meetings with your board members' consent.

Sample Advisory Meeting Agenda

Below is a sample agenda to help you get started and plan for your first advisory meeting:

06:00 – 06:10 Introduction and Overview

Introduce yourself and/or your management. Introduce advisory board members to each other. Then, provide a brief update on the current status of the business, the specific challenges or opportunities to address, and any approaches or solutions being considered.

06:10 – 06:30 Role and Expectations from the Advisory Board

Briefly discuss the Advisory Board's mandate or purpose and how the board can support the entrepreneur or management in general and in terms of the specific points for today's discussion. You can also include a brief orientation of policies and procedures such as attendance, frequency and schedule of meetings, discussion procedures, criteria for selection and voting, etc.

06:30 – 06:45 Questions from the Board

06:45 – 07:00 Presentation of Topic no. 1

Includes a brief description, discussion of materials and any presentation necessary, as well as questioning to assure the topic and associated caveats are clear and understood.

07:00 – 07:45 Discussion and Input

Generation of ideas, viewpoints and contributions from board members as well as yourself or management

07:45 – 08:00 Proposals and Evaluation

Review and selection of the best strategies or solutions to the issue in discussion

08:00 – 08:10   Summary of Topic, Discussion, and Action Plans

08:10 – 08:30   Presentation of Topic no. 2

08:30 – 09:00   Discussion and Input

09:00 – 09:15   Proposals and Evaluation

09:15 – 09:20   Summary of Topic, Discussion, and Action Plans

09:30 – 10:00   Adjournment
Includes announcement of next scheduled meeting and any expected actions or results from board members

You get the idea…..

-**Note:** In future meetings make sure to start by reviewing the topics and action plans that were discussed and agreed upon when you last convened, and then brief your board on the results and actions carried out by your company.

CHAPTER V

PLANNING FOR LONG TERM GROWTH

Over the coming months and years, you will find yourself more and more involved in the continuous yet enjoyable process of interacting with your advisory board and utilizing their guidance, connections and advice in accelerating your business.

But you may also find this to be overwhelming as you now have a powerful team to manage. This is where advisory boards can be helpful as well – helping you to be better at managing your time. We would highly recommend that you read "The 10 Natural Laws of Successful Time and Life Management" by Hyrum W. Smith. This book will change your life as a business owner for the better.

You will find over time that you may need to:

- Review and revise the mandate of your advisory board

- Evaluate the performance of your team and each adviser

- Recruit, renew or replace your board members

- Continuously improve communication and meeting procedures

- Strengthen accountability and expectation of results from board members

- Review compensation packages

The overall aim is to sharpen your advisory board and make it continuously active, productive, and more effective.

Here are just a few last-minute tips to help you successfully maintain and manage your advisory board in the long-term

1. Regular meetings and keeping your advisors consistently in the loop is the bread and butter that will sustain and keep your advisory board alive and kicking. Do not allow your advisory board to go into long periods of hibernation.

2. Keep your advisors enthusiastic and excited by giving them regular monthly or biweekly updates about your business, the latest news, acquisitions, reductions, expansions and any changes. Even if your meetings are not scheduled until a month or so from now, keep your members in the loop, even if you don't yet need their advice.

3. Respect your advisory board's inputs by appreciating their feedback, considering their recommendations and implementing solutions from your board meetings that your company agrees to approve. Inform your board members of

the status and progress of resolutions agreed upon from previous meetings or one-on-one discussions.

4. Listen, listen, listen. Listen to what your advisors say. Your relationship with each of your advisors should be one that encourages free and honest communication. Do not discourage your advisors from providing you with frank, objective feedback.

5. Employ technology whenever it can do the trick. Respect your advisors' time by opting to hold conference calls, email, chat, or video conferencing instead when convening may not be possible.

6. Eliminate non-productive board members if you feel you have made a bad choice. Do not waste your resources on advisors who do not add value to your board or your business as a whole. Alternatively, do not renew their advisory terms.

CONCLUSION

We hope we have helped equip you with the key tools you need in planning and creating a terrific advisory board. As you utilize this powerful and cost-effective resource, we are confident you will happily enjoy the benefits of an increased network reach, instant access to expertise and invaluable advice that your advisors provide. We wish you, your business and your advisory board continued and even greater success!

There are no magic formulas, or short cuts to this work we do as entrepreneurs. It is a continuous learning process, and if we can look ourselves in the mirror every day and honestly assess our own shortfalls and limitations, we can identify the areas we need to fill with competent people or "advisors." Advisors are just people, and if chosen correctly, they are people who will make up for our own limitations and that will be reflected in our businesses.

This isn't about our business as much as it is about ourselves. The business is a reflection of ourselves, and all of our strengths AND weaknesses. The hardest thing to do is to be honest with ourselves in where our limitations are, and then finding the people to fill those gaps.

If we can be helpful in any other way, please do let us know by leaving a review. We wish you the best of luck and success in all that you do. We hope this guidebook provides you with the value that we intended.

Thanks for reading,

Arthur W.B. & The Advisory Board Group

Boston, MA

ABOUT THE AUTHOR

We are a group of entrepreneur/business owners, living in Boston, NYC, and London who look to fill gaps and support other entrepreneurs when we can.

We are fully engaged in building our own businesses for our own purposes.

We are not interested in acknowledgements or promotions from this book.

We simply saw a need, compiled the information in a simple format and published for other small business owners to benefit.

Our intent is that the price of this book is far lower than the value you received from it. This represents our view on adding value to the world – make sure the value exceeds the price you paid for it.

Believe in yourself and believe in others.

Learn from your failures and never lose enthusiasm.

☺

Made in United States
Orlando, FL
01 May 2022

17399650R00061